COOL COLLECTIONS

Can You See What I See?

COOL COLLECTIONS

PICTURE PUZZLES TO SEARCH AND SOLVE

by Walter Wick

SCHOLASTIC INC.

New York   Toronto   London   Auckland   Mexico City   Sydney

New Delhi   Hong Kong   Buenos Aires

Published by Scholastic Inc.

SCHOLASTIC, CARTWHEEL BOOKS, and

associated logos are trademarks and/or

registered trademarks of Scholastic Inc.

ISBN: 0-439-61772-3

10 9 8 7 6   10 11 12 /0

Printed in Singapore 46

First printing, September 2004

Book Design by Walter Wick and David Saylor

FOR JORDAN ZWETCHKENBAUM

Library of Congress Cataloging-in-Publication Data

Wick, Walter.

Can you see what I see? Cool collections: picture puzzles to search

and solve / by Walter Wick.   p. cm.

Summary: Readers search for objects hidden in photographs of buttons,

dinosaurs, robots, shells, cars, animals, leaves, beads, game pieces, and the

contents of a junk drawer.

ISBN 0-439-61772-3 (hard cover)

1. Picture puzzles—Juvenile literature. [1. Picture puzzles.] I. Title: Cool Collections.

II. Title.   GV1507.P47W512 2004   793.73--dc22

2004002650

CONTENTS

Can you see

what I see?

An owl, a bear,

a baseball bat,

a butterfly,

a duck in a hat,

a purple teapot,

2 dice, 2 dogs,

a red sailboat,

3 bunnies, 3 frogs,

a palm tree, a shell,

5 anchors, a pail,

an elephant's trunk,

a dinosaur's tail!

Can you see
what I see?
2 dinosaurs
with outstretched wings,
a snake with spots,
a snake with rings,
a turtle, a snail,
a shark in a pool,
4 skeletons,
a pencil, a spool,
a crayon, a brush,
a bottle of glue,
a dragonfly,
a robot, too!

Can you see
what I see?
A hammer, a fork,
a 1, 2, 3,
a police car
with a windup key,
a horseshoe magnet,
a lobster claw,
a DANGER sign,
a saw, a straw,
a soup-can robot
that's ringing a bell,
a whistle, a teapot,
a silver seashell!

Can you see
what I see?
5 starfish, a feather,
a button that's green,
a red lobster claw,
the number 13,
a one-cent coin,
a bug on a board,
2 ants, a fly,
a pirate's sword,
a lock, a key,
a rubber duck,
a bottle cap,
a car, a truck!

Can you see
what I see?
A popped-up hood,
an open door,
a race car
with the number 4,
a checkered flag,
a truck for mail,
a traffic cone,
a car for sale,
a motorbike,
a plane, a plow,
a horse's head,
3 ducks, a cow!

19

Can you see
what I see?
A goose in a hat,
a sleepy dog,
a cow on a sign,
a princely frog,
5 polar bears,
4 kangaroos,
a balancing ball,
2 horseshoes,
a moose, a mouse,
a banana thief,
a bunny rabbit,
a red fall leaf.

Can you see
what I see?
5 bird feathers,
3 flowerpots,
a stone with stripes,
a stone with spots,
a jack-o'-lantern,
7 acorns,
3 seedpods
with prickly thorns,
a squirrel, a spider,
8 pumpkin seeds,
a dragonfly wing,
a strand of beads.

Can you see
what I see?
A cowboy boot,
a windmill, a fan,
a crack on a bell,
grapes in a can,
a ball with stitches,
a name with an E,
a buffalo nickel,
a domino 3,
a horse, a carriage,
2 hats, 2 mittens,
a comb, a lock,
3 bears, 3 kittens.

Can you see
what I see?
2 roosters, a stork,
a tiger, a crow,
a skunk, 2 frogs,
a polka-dot bow,
a hat made of straw,
a bunny that's blue,
a mouse, an eagle,
a butterfly, too,
a safety pin,
a heart-shaped lock,
2 soccer balls,
a bear on a block!

CHOCK-A-BLOCK

Can you see
what I see?
A faucet, a fence,
a lamp, 5 candles,
a turtle, a trolley,
a cart with 2 handles,
3 green trees,
a curvy kite tail,
2 fishing poles,
a parrot, a pail,
a red parachute,
a squirrel, 5 mice,
4 camels, a cow,
2 checkers, 3 dice!

Can you see
what I see?
A question mark,
a dollar sign,
a frog, a fly,
a fishing line,
a jack-in-the-box,
an oilcan,
a pocketbook,
a folding fan,
a dragon's tail,
an elephant's trunk,
a mail car,
a sack of junk!

Can you see
what I see?
A beach umbrella,
a car, 2 ships,
a safety pin,
3 paper clips,
a sword, a soldier,
a jet, a jack,
4 locks, 5 keys,
a blue thumbtack,
a jingle bell,
an arrowhead,
a button that's green,
a button that's red!

My photography in the Can You See What I See? and the I Spy books often inspires readers to ask, "Where do you get all the stuff?" Since *Cool Collections* was conceived as a celebration of "stuff," it seems appropriate to answer that question here.

The big yellow marble that appears in "Games Galore," as well as in the cover photography also appears in a picture I took more than twenty years ago. It may even be a toy from my childhood. But I acquired most of my collection since 1991, when I started to work on children's books.

I began my collection simply by scavenging junk drawers. Every family has one. In my opinion, a junk drawer is nothing to be embarrassed about. As a kid, it was the place I went to find tools, missing toy parts, and most importantly, inspiration for build-it-yourself projects. A proper junk drawer needs a little jostling to open and some deft rearranging of its overstuffed contents to close.

I continued to collect objects at yard sales, flea markets, and antique fairs. At such places I've found boxes full of toy cars; mason jars full of marbles, beads, and buttons; tin containers with toy blocks; and much, much more. Discount shops, party supply stores, craft supply stores, hardware stores, and of course, toy stores are also favorite sources. And finally, I get some things for free: from walks on beaches and in the woods.

Needless to say, my collection has grown very large and I have spent a great deal of time organizing it. Thus, years of sorting and re-sorting objects into such categories as blocks, beads, buttons, shells, rocks, zoo animals, woodland animals, birds, fish, dinosaurs, antique games, cars, etc., no doubt inspired *Cool Collections*. I love this stuff. I hope you do, too!

Acknowledgments

To Dan Helt and Kim Wildey, for their help with photography, set construction, and prop management; to my wife, Linda Cheverton-Wick, for her inspiration and encouragement; to my editor, Grace Maccarone, for her guidance, and art director Rich Deas, for his design expertise; to Nancy Morgan, for lending me stuffed animals for "Plush Passions," and Michael Lokensgaard, for giving me access to his robot and space toy collections; to Lois Diehm and Donna Amurso, for their enthusiastic support, my heartfelt thanks.　— Walter Wick

Walter Wick is the photographer of the I Spy series of books, with more than nine million copies in print. He is author and photographer of *A Drop of Water: A Book of Science and Wonder*, which won the Boston Globe/Horn Book Award for Nonfiction, was named a Notable Children's Book by the American Library Association, and was selected as an Orbis Pictus Honor Book and a CBC/NSTA Outstanding Science Trade Book for Children. *Walter Wick's Optical Tricks*, a book of photographic illusions, was named a Best Illustrated Children's Book by the *New York Times Book Review*, was recognized as a Notable Children's Book by the American Library Association, and received many awards, including a Platinum Award from the Oppenheim Toy Portfolio, a Young Readers Award from *Scientific American*, a *Bulletin* Blue Ribbon, and a Parents' Choice Silver Honor. *Can You See What I See?*, published in 2003, appeared on the *New York Times* Best-seller List for twenty-two weeks. His most recent books in the Can You See What I See? series are *Dream Machine* and *Seymour and the Juice Box Boat*. Mr. Wick has invented photographic games for *GAMES* magazine and photographed covers for books and magazines, including *Newsweek, Discover,* and *Psychology Today*. A graduate of Paier College of Art, Mr. Wick lives in Connecticut with his wife, Linda.